SETTING
THE STAGE
FOR FLUENCY

Follow the Drinking Gourd

Come Along the Underground Railroad

by Wim Coleman and Pat Perrin
illustrated by Courtney A. Martin

RED
CHAIR
•PRESS•

Please visit our website at **www.redchairpress.com** for more high-quality products for young readers.

 EDUCATORS: Find FREE lesson plans and a Readers' Theater script for this book at www.redchairpress.com/free-activities.

About the Authors

Wim Coleman and **Pat Perrin** are a husband and wife who write together. Their more-than-100 publications include plays, stories, articles, essays, books, classroom materials, and mainstream fiction. Wim has a BFA in Theatre Arts and an MAT in English and Education from Drake University. Pat has a BA in English from Duke, an MA in Liberal Studies from Hollins University, and a PhD in Art Theory and Criticism from the University of Georgia. Both have classroom teaching experience. For 13 years they lived in the beautiful Mexican town of San Miguel de Allende, where they created and managed a scholarship program for at-risk students under the auspices of San Miguel PEN. Some of their stories draw on Mexican myth and tradition. Their highly-praised works for young readers include award-winning historical fiction, popular collections of plays, and a "nonfiction" book about unicorns.

Follow The Drinking Gourd: Come Along the Underground Railroad

Publisher's Cataloging-In-Publication Data
(Prepared by The Donohue Group, Inc.)

Coleman, Wim.
Follow the Drinking Gourd : come along the Underground Railroad / by Wim Coleman and Pat Perrin ; illustrated by Courtney A. Martin.

p. : ill. ; cm. -- (Setting the stage for fluency)

Summary: A dramatization of two escaped slaves who share their brave story along the path to freedom called the Underground Railroad. Includes special book features for further study and a special section for teachers and librarians.
Interest age level: 009-012.
Includes bibliographical references.
ISBN: 978-1-939656-11-7 (lib. binding/hardcover)
ISBN: 978-1-939656-10-0 (pbk.)
ISBN: 978-1-939656-12-4 (eBk)

1. Underground Railroad--Juvenile drama. 2. Fugitive slaves--United States--History--Juvenile drama. 3. Slavery--United States--History--Juvenile drama. 4. Underground Railroad--Drama. 5. Fugitive slaves--United States--History--Drama. 6. Slavery--United States--History--Drama. 7. Children's plays, American. I. Perrin, Pat. II. Martin, Courtney A. III. Title.

PS3553.O47448 Fo 2014
[Fic]   2013956250

This series first published by:
Red Chair Press LLC   PO Box 333   South Egremont, MA 01258-0333

Printed in the United States of America

1 2 3 4 5 18 17 16 15 14

TABLE OF CONTENTS

INTRODUCTION

A slave is a person who is the legal property of another person. Slavery in the United States became illegal in the 1860s. Before that, some free people who were opposed to slavery helped slaves escape. This play is about a brother and sister who escape slavery.

The play begins in 1880 with Old Ellie and Old Sam. They are the narrators who tell how they escaped years before. Young Ellie and Young Sam are the escaping slaves. Their story takes place in 1855–1856.

Many slaves found their way north by following Polaris, the North Star.

They looked first for the Big Dipper, which they called the Drinking Gourd. The two front stars of the Big Dipper point towards Polaris — and toward freedom.

The path they followed and the people who helped were called the "Underground Railroad."

THE CAST OF CHARACTERS

You'll notice that Old Ellie and Old Sam, living in 1880, are the narrators. Young Sam and Young Ellie are featured in the flashbacks.

Old Ellie, Narrator

Old Sam, Narrator

Smith, a white plantation worker

Mr. Burkett, a white plantation owner

Young Sam, an African-American boy, age 12

Young Ellie, an African-American girl (Sam's sister), age 14

Peg Leg Joe, a white traveling carpenter

Amy, an African-American girl, age 7

Angela, Amy's mother

Lucy, Amy's sister, age 10

Slave Hunters, 1, 2, 3, and 4

Zeke, a free African-American man

SCENE ONE

Old Ellie: When the sun comes back…

Old Sam: And the first **quail** calls…

Old Ellie & Old Sam: Follow the drinking **gourd**.

Old Ellie: Oh, I don't think I'll forget those words if I live to be a hundred.

Old Sam: I sure do remember the first time we ever heard them.

Old Ellie: Some 25 years ago it was, back on a cold February evening in 1855. We were down in deepest Alabama.

Smith: *(shouting over barking hounds)* It's getting dark, Mr. Burkett.

Mr. Burkett: We'll find them. They can't have gone more than a mile.

Old Sam: We had run off from the Burkett **plantation**, down near Jackson.

Old Ellie: Old man Burkett and his overseer, Smith, were after us in no time flat. They searched the whole countryside with **bloodhounds**.

Mr. Burkett: I can get a good three or four years of hard labor out of them—if they don't die from the whipping I'll give them. Let loose the hounds, Smith, and head after them. I'll wait here.

Smith: Yes, sir!

Old Ellie: We were hiding behind a fallen tree trunk, listening.

Young Sam: The men don't scare me so much. It's the hounds that do.

Young Ellie: Over **yonder**'s a creek. If we can get into it before they catch us, we stand a chance.

Young Sam: How?

Young Ellie: Hounds can't sniff out a scent through water. Come on. Let's go, and fast! But stay stooped down low.

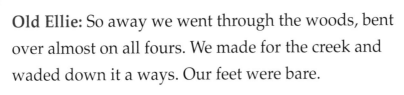

Old Ellie: So away we went through the woods, bent over almost on all fours. We made for the creek and waded down it a ways. Our feet were bare.

Young Sam: The water's so cold!

Young Ellie: Stop your fussing! Let's wade out and hide behind that brush.

Old Sam: We hid and then peeked out through the twigs.

Young Ellie: *(whispering)* Here come the hounds. See? They're only going to the edge of the creek.

Young Sam: *(whispering)* And here comes Smith behind them.

Young Ellie: *(whispering)* Poor dogs, sniffing up and down the creek bank, all puzzled-like.

Smith: You dumb mutts, where are they? Old man Burkett will tan all our hides if we go back to him empty-handed.

Young Sam: *(whispering)* Look! Three of those hounds are sniffing their ways upstream!

Young Ellie: *(whispering)* And the other three are sniffing their ways on down.

Old Sam: And dumb old Smith didn't know what to make of it!

Old Ellie: We stayed on our bellies so he wouldn't see us. Away we crawled like a pair of snakes. We crawled and crawled and crawled, until—

Young Sam: I don't hear the barking anymore.

Young Ellie: Me neither. **Reckon** it's safe to get up on our feet.

Young Sam: My, but the nighttime's come on in a hurry.

Young Ellie: Stars sure are bright, though. And a big full moon's out.

Young Sam: What do we do now, Ellie?

Young Ellie: We'd best catch some sleep. Look over in that field. There's a big fat haystack. It'll make a nice bed, I reckon.

Young Sam: Nicer than we've had in a long time.

Old Sam: So we headed for that haystack. We dug our way inside it and let our tired bones go limp.

Old Ellie: We fell asleep before we knew it. Hard to say how long we slept.

Old Sam: But that singing… it was the singing that woke us up.

Peg Leg Joe: *(singing)*
> When the sun comes back,
> And the first quail calls,
> Follow the Drinking Gourd.

Young Sam: Ellie, you hear that?

Young Ellie: *(whispering)* Shhh! *(pauses)* The singing's stopped.

Young Sam: *(whispering)* D'you reckon whoever's singing went off somewhere?

Young Ellie: *(whispering)* No. I still hear his footsteps.

Young Sam: *(whispering)* Those don't sound like regular footsteps.

Young Ellie: *(whispering)* You're right. They're like a step and a crunch, a step and a crunch, a step and a crunch.

Old Ellie: My teeth were chattering so hard in my head, I thought he'd hear them.

Old Sam: Then all of a sudden, a pair of strong, rough hands grabbed hold of my ankles. I was yanked clear out into the open air!

Young Sam: Hey!

Old Ellie: The same hands grabbed me by the wrists, yanking me out with you.

Young Ellie: Hey!

Peg Leg Joe: Well, well. What have we got here?

Old Sam: As we stood in the moonlight, we got a good look at him. He was a tall, old white man with a gray beard.

Old Ellie: His right leg was lopped off at the knee, and he wore a wooden peg instead. He had a bag hung over his shoulder.

Peg Leg Joe: Looks like I've uncovered me a nest of escaped slave children.

Young Sam: There's only two of us, honest.

Young Ellie: Don't turn us in, mister, please!

Young Sam: We're likely to get whipped to death.

Peg Leg Joe: Why should I care about that? And why shouldn't I collect a big reward for turning you in? Dumb little pups! Hiding in the wide open under a stack of hay! What if a band of slave hunters comes this way with a pack of hounds? That's the first place they'd look! Do you have any food for traveling?

Young Sam: *(very surprised)* No, sir.

Peg Leg Joe: Got yourselves good walking shoes?

Young Ellie: *(equally surprised)* No, sir.

Peg Leg Joe: Too dumb to live, the both of you. Let's see if I've got anything here.

Old Ellie: The old man started digging around in his bag.

Peg Leg Joe: Got some dried fruit here. Some strips of smoked beef. A little bit of bread. You can fill this flask up from a creek. Just be sure the water 's fit for drinking.

Old Sam: He handed us a flat metal bottle with a top.

Peg Leg Joe: Got an old bandana to tie everything up in. Here you go.

Young Sam: Thank you kindly, mister.

Peg Leg Joe: I got one more thing for you—a little song: *(singing)*

> When the sun comes back,
> And the first quail calls,
> Follow the Drinking Gourd.
> For the old man is a-waiting
> To carry you to freedom,
> If you follow the Drinking Gourd.

Young Sam: That's a right pretty song.

Peg Leg Joe: It's more than just a song, son. It's a riddle. If you can guess it, here's what will happen. You'll get on a big, fine railroad train. One of its stops will be a little house with a white flag waving in the front yard. Go straight to the front door and knock. Somebody will let you in—somebody a whole lot nicer than me. You kids be careful, now.

Young Sam: There he goes—and I'm glad he's gone!

Young Ellie: But he did give us something to eat.

Young Sam: Yeah, but he's plumb crazy.

Young Ellie: Maybe not so crazy. We might solve his riddle yet. Look there at the sky.

Old Sam: Ellie pointed, tracing a shape in the stars.

Young Ellie: There's a handle, and a gourd-shaped cup.

Young Sam: A drinking gourd!

Young Ellie: And those two stars on the cup, they point to that bright star over yonder.

Young Sam: I see it.

Young Ellie: That's the North Star. It's always in the north part of the sky—north, where they say there's freedom.

Young Sam: "Follow the Drinking Gourd." Like in the song!

Young Ellie: That's just what we're going to do. Follow it to freedom.

Old Ellie: Oh, it was cold. But we **trudged** on all that night over hills, through woods, across creeks and fields. We never took our eyes off that star.

Old Sam: We got hungry by and by and snacked on the old man's food. But we never stopped moving.

Old Ellie: We kept walking even after the sun was up and we heard birds singing.

Young Ellie: Sam! You hear that song? "Bob-WHITE. Bob-WHITE." That's the quail's song.

Young Sam: The quail comes through these parts this time of year. "When the sun comes back and the first quail calls…"

Young Ellie: And dawn's coming earlier every morning because winter's wearing on. The sun's coming back! That's what the old man's song is saying. It's saying that winter is the right time of year for escaping north!

Young Sam: It's powerful cold, though. If I could do the choosing, I'd go escaping in the summer.

Young Ellie: Oh, Sam! Look there, over yonder. There's a little log cabin, with a wisp of smoke coming out of its chimney. And in the front yard there's a white handkerchief tied to a twig!

Young Sam: It's a flag, just like the old man said. But where's the big old railroad train we're supposed to be on?

Young Ellie: Maybe the train comes later. He said there's someone friendly in that cabin. Let's go knock at the door.

Old Sam: Ellie went running across the meadow to the cabin, and I sure wasn't going to let her go alone. I took off after her as fast as I could go.

Young Ellie: *(calling)* Is anybody home?

Old Sam: A little black girl, maybe 7 years old, opened the door just a crack. She peeked out shyly.

Young Ellie: Hello, little punkin. What's your name?

Amy: Amy.

Young Ellie: Are your folks at home?

Amy: My mama is here and my big sister. Come in.

Old Ellie: We walked inside the little one-room cabin. It was the coziest place we ever did see. It had a real wood floor. A big fire was roaring in the stone fireplace, and a pot of stew was simmering over it.

Old Sam: A young woman and a girl sat at an oak table. They were stitching away at a mess of clothes. A big pile of them was already done. The woman didn't seem surprised to see us.

Angela: I see we have visitors. My name's Angela, and this is my older daughter, Lucy. You've already met my little one.

Lucy: How d'you do?

Young Ellie: Fine, thank you.

Angela: Fine? You look right tired. Escaping, are you?

Young Sam: From the Burkett place.

Young Ellie: Master Burkett took to hitting my little brother lately. I reckoned we didn't have any choice and no time left. So we just lit out.

Angela: Have yourselves a seat. I'll serve us all some stew soon as I finish this hem.

Old Sam: Angela told us that she and her daughters got freed by their master in his will when he died. Ever since, they'd taken to helping escaped slaves.

Old Ellie: They knew Peg Leg Joe. They told us about him, at least all anybody knew—just that he was an old traveling carpenter who kept going from one plantation to another, helping slaves get free.

Old Sam: Angela and the girls fixed us up with new clothes and shoes stitched together from cowhide.

Old Ellie: Then we all sat down to eat some nice hot stew and talk some more.

Angela: Some good food and a bit of rest is what you need. You'll need your strength for the railroad.

Young Sam: Railroad?

Young Ellie: Peg Leg Joe told us about a railroad.

Young Sam: Where is it?

Angela: *(chuckling)* Well, listen carefully now while we teach you another verse of Peg Leg's song.

Angela, Amy, Lucy: *(singing)*
> The riverbank makes a very good road,
> The dead trees show you the way.
> Left foot, peg foot, traveling on,
> Follow the Drinking Gourd.

Lucy: Mama! I hear galloping horses!

Old Ellie: Angela peeked through her window curtain.

Angela: There are two of them, riding straight this way. Children, your master seems to want you back real bad. You've got to light out of here real fast.

Amy: Come over here.

Old Sam: The girls led us to the back of the cabin. They pulled up a couple of loose floorboards.

Amy: We've dug out a little passage under here. Crawl out back behind the house. The woods are close by. You can get there without anyone seeing you.

Burkett: *(shouting)* Open up! I know you've got my runaways in there!

Angela: Nobody's here but me and my girls! Go away and mind your business.

Lucy: *(to Sam and Ellie)* Go! Now!

Old Sam: And down we went, right under the cabin floor. The girls slammed the floorboards back in place. Then we heard the door fly open and footsteps stomp in the cabin.

Burkett: Where are they? Where's my property?

Angela: You see anybody here except me and my children?

Old Ellie: We **scrambled** up outside the back of the cabin into the daylight.

Young Sam: Oh, Ellie. Do you think Angela and the girls will be all right in there?

Young Ellie: They've done this before, that's sure. Anyways, there's nothing we can do for them now. Come on!

Old Ellie: We headed for the woods.

Old Sam: Soon we got clean out of sight of the cabin.

Old Ellie: We didn't even know which way it was we ran. It was just dumb luck we didn't get ourselves lost and caught.

Old Sam: But pretty soon, we came to a river—the Tombigbee River, it was.

Young Ellie: Remember what the song said, Sam?

Young Sam: *"The riverbank makes a very good road."*

Young Ellie: That means we should follow it. But do we follow it upstream or down?

Young Sam: We got to keep going north.

Young Ellie: But the sun's all covered with clouds. I can't tell which way's which. Does this river flow north or south?

Young Sam: Look at this dead tree here. Something's carved in its bark.

Young Ellie: It looks like somebody's foot.

Young Sam: And look just beyond it. There's another piece of dead wood with something carved on it.

Young Ellie: Why, it's a peg leg, as sure as can be!

Young Sam: And there's a foot carved on a branch a little farther along.

Young Ellie: And another peg leg, just past that. Remember the song?

Young Sam: *"Left foot, peg foot, traveling on."*

Young Ellie: Somebody carved us a trail to follow! These signs surely show that north is upstream. That's where we've got to go.

Old Ellie: So away we ran, upstream along the Tombigbee River.

Old Sam: For the first week or so, we slept under leaves along the riverbank or in barns or stables.

Old Ellie: By and by, folks along the way gave us food and shelter. Free black people and friendly white people all helped us along.

Old Sam: The white folks acted near as brave as the black folks. They could have wound up in jail or something worse if they'd got caught.

Old Ellie: We learned a lot during those months traveling.

Old Sam: We learned that moss always grows on the north side of a tree.

Old Ellie: We learned it was safer traveling nights than days.

Old Sam: And, oh, we learned lots of signs and signals.

Old Ellie: A candle was burning in a second-story window. That meant the family who lived there was friendly.

Old Sam: We even learned about messages in quilts. We'd see them hanging from clotheslines or in windows.

Old Ellie: I remember one day in the fall, near Aberdeen, Mississippi. We'd come alongside some railroad tracks.

Young Ellie: Oh, little brother, do you hear that sound?

Young Sam: It's a train whistle, sure enough.

Young Ellie: Do you reckon it's that railroad train we heard about?

Young Sam: Maybe it'll stop and pick us up!

Young Ellie: *(sadly)* It ain't slowing down—not even a speck.

Young Sam: Nobody but white folks riding it, as far as I can see. Reckon it's not our train, Ellie.

Young Ellie: That's too bad. My feet do get tired from all this walking!

Young Sam: It sure would be nice, taking a nice warm train at least some of the way.

Young Ellie: I wonder if we'll ever find that railroad.

SCENE FOUR

Peg Leg Joe: *(singing)*

> The riverbank makes a very good road,
> The dead trees show you the way.

Old Sam: I'll never forget when we heard that old voice singing once again.

Old Ellie: Me neither. Fall had come, and the leaves were gone. The days were getting right cold again.

Young Sam: Listen, Ellie. It's him! Peg Leg Joe!

Young Ellie: I hear wheels turning.

Young Sam: There he is, up on the road, driving his wagon along.

Young Ellie: *(shouting)* Peg Leg Joe! Peg Leg Joe!

Old Sam: He pulled his wagon to a stop. It was all loaded up with wooden furniture he'd made.

Peg Leg Joe: Hush up, you fools! You want to bring every slave hunter in the territory down on us? Look at this paper. It's a wanted poster. Do you know these faces?

Young Ellie: Why, it's us!

Peg Leg Joe: A certain Mr. Aaron Burkett down in Alabama is right anxious to get the two of you back. He's offered a $100 reward for each of your **scrawny carcasses**. These papers are posted up all over every town in this part of the country. Why, I'm almost tempted to turn you in myself. Climb up in back and get yourselves hid!

Old Sam: So we climbed into an empty cabinet in the back of his wagon. We went rattling on down the road while Peg Leg sang some more.

Peg Leg Joe: *(singing)*
     The river ends between two hills,
     Follow the Drinking Gourd.
     There's another river on the other side,
     Follow the Drinking Gourd.

Old Sam: I peeked out through the crack between the cabinet doors.

Young Ellie: What do you seen, Sam?

Young Sam: We're driving through a valley. The river's nothing more than a trickle. And we're between two hills, sure enough.

Old Ellie: After a while, the wagon ground to a stop.

Peg Leg Joe: *(singing)* There's another river on the other side, Follow the Drinking Gourd.
(speaking) Now, out with you two!

Old Sam: We climbed out of the wagon and found ourselves facing a river.

Old Ellie: The Tennessee River, it was.

Young Ellie: We owe you a lot, mister.

Peg Leg Joe: Yes, you do! But get along now. Don't let me see you for a real long time.

Old Ellie: He snapped his reins and rode off, singing as he went.

Peg Leg Joe: *(singing)*
>Where the great big river meets the little river,
>Follow the Drinking Gourd.
>For the old man is a-waiting to carry you to freedom
>If you follow the Drinking Gourd.

Young Sam: What do we do now, Ellie?

Young Ellie: Well, the song's pretty clear. It says there's a "little river" and a "big river," and the two rivers meet. We've got to follow this little river upstream till it meets a big river.

Young Sam: More walking, then! I do wish we could get on that railroad!

SCENE FIVE

Old Ellie: In the days ahead, we often wished we could get on that railroad.

Old Sam: We traveled for two more months following the Tennessee River.

Old Ellie: The winter hit us hard. Remember?

Old Sam: Every few nights, some kindly soul would take us in. They'd give us a hot meal to eat and a roof to sleep under.

Old Ellie: But we spent way too many nights trying to stay warm. We often slept under a pile of leaves by the riverbank.

Old Sam: Then came one bright, clear, cold night in early January. The river had already turned to a big sheet of ice…

Young Ellie: Oh, look yonder, little brother! This little river of ours runs right into a great big river! Just like the song says.

Young Sam: That sure is the biggest river I ever did see! My, how all that ice glitters in the moonlight, like it's twinkling stars.

Young Ellie: And over across the ice, on that point of land where the two rivers meet—

Young Sam: Why, there's a big fire burning there.

Young Ellie: And there's a man standing beside it.

Young Sam: He's waving his arms. Do you reckon he's waving at us?

Young Ellie: He sees us in the moonlight. I think he wants us to come walking across the ice.

Young Sam: Do you reckon it's safe?

Young Ellie: It's got to be. We don't have a choice. Come on, let's go.

Old Ellie: So we started walking across the ice.

Old Sam: It was slippery and cold under our feet.

Young Sam: Oh, Ellie—what's that groaning sound?

Young Ellie: That's the ice creaking under us.

Young Sam: Can it hold us?

Young Ellie: It ought to. We're neither one of us much more than skin and bone.

Old Ellie: We were halfway across when we heard voices behind us.

Slave hunter 1: Hey, there!

Slave hunter 2: You two children! Stop where you are!

Slave hunter 1: Stop, or we'll shoot!

Young Sam: They've got guns!

Young Ellie: They won't shoot us. We're worth too much alive.

Young Sam: *(hearing a shot fired)* You thought wrong, big sister!

Young Ellie: That bullet whizzed right by my ear!

Young Sam: Seems like they'd rather get us dead than not at all!

Young Ellie: Keep on moving—slow and steady now. *(hearing the ice break)* Don't start running, or you're likely to bust the ice.

Old Sam: Then we heard a crashing noise behind us.

Young Sam: What's that sound?

Young Ellie: Don't look back! Keep your eyes straight ahead!

Old Sam: But I couldn't help glancing over my shoulder. The men were bigger and heavier than we were. They'd been all bunched up close together. A hole had broken through the ice, and one of the men was in the water.

Slave hunter 1: Help! I've fallen in! Get me out of here.

Old Ellie: We kept moving. By and by, we were climbing up the riverbank.

Old Sam: The old man who had waved towered over us in the firelight. He looked out over the ice.

Zeke: *(chuckling)* Look at that poor devil yonder! He's soaked to the skin in this freezing weather. He's likely to catch his death of cold.

Old Ellie: I looked back across the river. The one man had pulled his friend out of that hole in the ice. Now they were limping their way back to the far shore.

Young Ellie: They won't be following us now, that's sure.

Zeke: My name's Zeke. You might have heard of me in a song.

Young Ellie: "For the old man is a-waiting to carry you to freedom."

Zeke: I'm that old man. Welcome to Indiana.

Young Ellie: Indiana! Why, that's a free state—right?

Young Sam: We're free now?

Zeke: No more free here than down South.

Young Ellie: How can that be?

Zeke: There's a law called the fugitive slave law. It says folks up North got to send escaped slaves back down South. They got to return slaves to their masters. Some folks up here are just as likely to turn you in as Southern folk. And slave hunters are all over these parts. Free folks can get into a mess of trouble trying to help runaway slaves.

Young Sam: Then what are we gonna do?

Zeke: You won't find proper freedom till you get over into Canada. My job's to help you along your way. Come on, get aboard the train.

Young Sam: Train? I don't see a train.

Young Ellie: Are we getting on the railroad at last?

Zeke: What do you mean "at last"? Where do you think you've been all this time? The friendly folks who helped, those were conductors. And the shelter those folks gave you were stations. And the pathways with signs and signals, those were tracks. Now the train's pulling out, so all aboard!

Old Ellie: So we took off after Zeke, walking through the cold.

Old Sam: But our feet didn't hurt so much—not after we knew the truth about the secret railroad.

WORDS TO KNOW

bloodhounds: dogs with a keen sense of smell

carcasses: bodies

gourd: a squash sometimes dried and carved out to scoop water

plantation: a large farm

quail: a kind of bird also called a bobwhite

reckon: guess or figure

scrambled: crawled in a hurry

scrawny: skinny

trudged: walked in a slow, tired way

yonder: there, in a distance

Learn More about the Underground Railroad

Books:

Hopkinson, Deborah. *Sweet Clara and the Freedom Quilt.* Dragonfly Books, 1993.

Levine, Ellen. *If You Travelled on the Underground Railroad.* Scholastic, 1993.

Lassieur, Allison. *The Underground Railroad: An Interactive History Adventure.* (You Choose Books) Capstone. 2007.

Web Sites:

An Interactive Journey from National Geographic Education:
http://tinyurl.com/mejwc9x

Places:

The National Underground Railroad **Freedom Center,** Cincinnati, Ohio.